Fifty Nifty FACTS ABOUT CATS

by J.M. Chapman & S.M. Davis

VULPINE PRESS

Published by Vulpine Press LLC
1400 N 30th Street, Quincy, IL 62301
www.vulpinepress.com
www.fiftyniftyfacts.com

ISBN-10:1-939276-51-9
ISBN-13:978-1-939276-51-3

Also available:

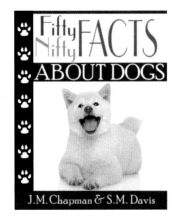

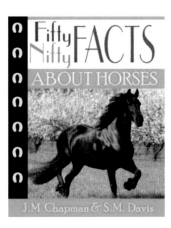

Cats dislike water because they get too wet.

A cat's furry coat does not repel water very well. When it gets wet, the cat gets soaked to the skin and may feel uncomfortable. Some cats like water, but usually a soggy kitty is an unhappy kitty.

2 Cats fit through spaces as big as their head.

Thanks to free-floating collar bones(attached only to muscle),
a cat's body is very flexible, making their heads the widest part.
They use their whiskers to test if they can fit through an opening.

Cats don't like sweets.

Their tongues lack sweet-sensing taste buds, so unlike humans and dogs, they don't care for sugar. In fact, as far as scientists know, felines are the only mammals without sweet taste buds.

3

4

Cats are warmer than people.

Cat internal temperature averages at 101.5 degrees Fahrenheit. Human body temperature averages 98.6 degrees. A cat's normal temperature would be considered a fever for a person.

Cats usually weigh about ten pounds.

The heaviest cat, Himmey from Australia, weighed 46 pounds.
That's more than the average six year old child!
The lightest adult cat on record weighed about 3 pounds.

6

Cats can only see certain colors.

Their eyes are great at seeing monochrome colors –
black, white, and gray, but can only see certain
colors—primarily muted shades of blue and green.

7

Cats use their tails for balance.

With 18-23 bones, cat tails vary in length—males typically have longer tails than females. The tail is used as a counterbalance to help cats walk on narrow beams and turn sharply when running.

8

Cat litters average 3-5 kittens.

Mother cats can have 2 or 3 litters of kittens per year.
The record for most kittens birthed in one litter is 19.
One cat named Dusty had 420 kittens in her lifetime.

9

Cats can sleep up to 20 hours a day.

Most of their sleep occurs as "cat"-napping. They doze lightly so they can wake quickly and spring into action if necessary. Cats sleep a lot to conserve energy for hunting.

10

Cats become lactose intolerant.

As a kitten ages, it loses the ability to digest the milk sugar, lactose. Ingesting dairy products, like milk and ice cream, can upset adult cats' bellies.

Cats seek high places.

By finding a suitably high perch, a cat can have a wide view of its territory while remaining safe from predators and scoping out its prey. They are superb hunters.

11

12

Cats show natural curiosity.

To feel safe and in control, a cat needs to know every potential hiding spot, danger or interesting object in the area they claim as their territory.

Cats always land on their feet.

Early in life, a cat develops a righting reflex, which automatically makes them turn feet down when falling. They do need a 12-inch drop to complete the turn.

14 Cats have a dominant paw.

Like humans, cats prefer to use one side of their body more than the other. Male cats tend to favor their left paw, while females prefer their right.

Cats walk in a narrow straight line.

Their strides take up little width, so that they can sneak through brush and narrow spaces. They need to make as little noise as possible while stalking their prey.

16

Cats need more than tuna.

Tuna offers a wide variety of nutrients necessary for a healthy life, but lacks the amino acid taurine. Without taurine in their diet, cats can go blind.

Cats are carnivores.

They require a diet of meat and only meat. Dry cat kibble often contains grains, and cats can't metabolize the carbs; long-term ingestion may cause diabetes.

18 Cats often get stuck in trees.

They seek high places to escape danger.
Hooked claws make climbing up a breeze, but
also require the cat to climb down backwards.

19

Cats have super sensitive whiskers.

Whiskers are touch receptors with many nerve endings. Located on a cat's face and wrists, whiskers can be used for navigation and testing openings.

20 Cats should not drink coffee.

Certain everyday chemicals are toxic to cats, including those found in coffee, chocolate, raisins, garlic, onions, and mushrooms.

Cats can be potty-trained.

Cats instinctively cover their wastes and thus prefer to go in a litter box. With proper training and patience, they can be taught to use the toilet.

21

22

Cats need to knead.

When cozy, a cat may knead, or rhythmically push its paws against soft objects. This is likely a soothing reminder of breastfeeding as a kitten.

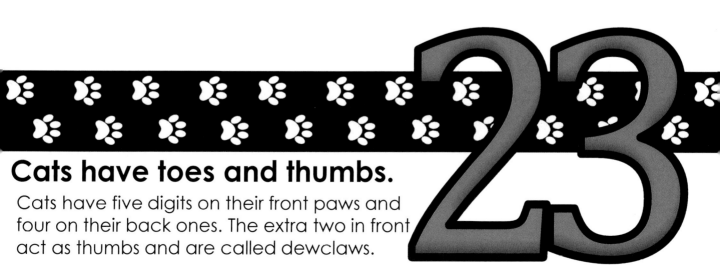

23

Cats have toes and thumbs.

Cats have five digits on their front paws and four on their back ones. The extra two in front act as thumbs and are called dewclaws.

24

Cats sweat.

If licking their fur is not enough to cool down, cats have sweat glands in their paws to vent more heat. Cats only pant when very hot.

Cats were worshipped in Egypt.

In ancient times, sphinxes were considered godly.
A pharaoh's cats were mummified alongside
them, and statues were created to honor them.

25

26

Cats are superfecund.

A single mom can have a litter with multiple fathers. Such a litter may have siblings that look very different from each other.

Cats can be hairless.

The first sphinx cat, now the most popular hairless breed, was born in Canada in 1966. Sphinxes aren't completely bald; their coats feel like suede.

27

28

Cats can be tailless.

Manx cats have a gene that results in no tail.
The gene isn't always fully expressed, so a litter
of manx kittens can have tails of various lengths.

29

Cats have been pets for ages.

Cats started living with people about 9,500 years ago—the same time humans started farming grains. Cats helped keep mice away.

30

Cats are the most popular pet.

A 2010 survey showed Americans had 86 million pet cats compared to 78 million pet dogs. More cats live in the USA than in any other country.

Cats have vertical, slit-shaped pupils.

31

Pupils allow light to enter the eye, so the animal can see. Cats have vertical pupils to help judge distance when pouncing on prey in the dark.

32

Cats live about thirteen years.

At least, indoor cats do. Outdoor cats have a shorter life expectancy of five years. The world's oldest cat, Cream Puff, lived to be 38!

Cats hear sounds in 11.5 octaves.

32 muscles move a cat's ear to pinpoint sounds.
Especially sensitive to high-pitched noises, they
can hear frequencies too high for dogs to hear.

33

34

Cats have two senses of smell.

Usually cats use the nose on their face, but they also have a Jacobson's organ in their mouth, which they mostly use to smell other cats' urine.

Cat spit can cause allergies.

Humans who are allergic to cats aren't allergic to their fur. They're allergic to a protein in cat saliva, which does get in their fur during grooming.

36 Cats have several types of hair.

Awn hairs form the basic coat; guard hairs determine cat color and form a water barrier; and the soft down undercoat provides warmth.

37

Cats' tongues are rough.

Abnormally long, backward-facing papillae give a cat's tongue a scrubbing texture. Cats spend half their awake-time grooming themselves.

38 Calico cats are female.

The gene for orange fur is on the X chromosome. Female cats have two X chromosomes (males have 1) which can result in fur with orange spots.

39

Cats go by many names.
In other languages: Katze (German), Popoki (Hawaiian), Mao (Chinese), Kissa (Finnish), & Neko (Japanese) A group of cats is a clowder, or if kittens, a kindle.

40

Cats have baby teeth.

Called deciduous teeth or milk teeth, kittens' first set of teeth starts to sprout at age three weeks and begins to fall out at four months.

Cats eat grass.

They don't digest it, but grass helps a cat regurgitate indigestible materials in their stomach including hairballs, bones, and feathers.

41

42

Cats only have one life.

It seems cats have nine lives, but their agility, anatomy, and dexterity allows them to survive high falls and other dangers that should kill them.

Cats purr for many reasons.

Usually, cats purr to express comfort. They might purr to ease tension or when they're injured. Purring has been found to stimulate bone regeneration!

43

44

Cats only meow at humans.

Kittens meow at their moms when hungry or cold, but adult cats don't meow at cats. Adults meow only at humans when seeking attention or food.

Cats hunt best at twilight.

Cats are crepuscular—most active at dusk and dawn—rather than nocturnal. Cat eyesight is acute in dim light, but not total darkness.

45

46

Cats can be polydactyl.

Cats can be born with extra unnecessary toes. One cat had 28 toes—7 per paw! Boston has more polydactyl cats than any other city.

Cats are extremely territorial.

Cats use scent glands on their tail, lips, forehead, front paws, and chin to rub their scent on their belongings, including humans. Males spray urine to mark territory.

47

48

Cats save human lives.

Cats hunt disease-carrying vermin. Half the people of Europe died in the 1300s when cats were outlawed and rats spread the plague.

Cats can drink seawater.

Drinking salt water dehydrates most mammals, but a cat's kidneys are so efficient, they can filter out the salt and rehydrate the body with seawater.

49

50

Cats' claws are retracted at rest.

Keeping claws covered when not in use for hunting, climbing or defense prevents the tip from wearing and catching on objects when walking.

Made in the
USA
Middletown, DE